Hiking Survival Guide

Conrad Blake

Basic Survival Kit and Necessary Survival Skills to Stay Alive in the Wilderness

ISBN-10: 1500943231

ISBN-13: 978-1500943233

Table of Contents

Let's Go Hiking

Hiking is one of the best forms of outdoor activity. You are walking in natural environments like forest or mountains, so it is more of a wilderness adventure than just a walk in the park. Being able to go hiking is one of life's great pleasures!

If you live near a good wilderness park, a deep canyon, a mountain, or a thick forest, hiking is a wonderful way to spend your weekend. Whether you go alone or with your family, you'll find that hiking is truly a joy!

Hiking benefits are both physical and mental. Studies have shown that people that spend time in nature tend to be more relaxed, less anxious, and less likely to suffer from stress-related disorders. Being out in the middle of nowhere is one of the best ways to get rid of work-week stress, so it's definitely worth considering going for a hike if you feel stressed.

If you're going hiking, you need to be aware of your surroundings. There are some dangers out there, and it's important that you know what you're getting yourself into. You also need to be prepared for accidents and emergency situations, as they can happen at any moment. If you're going to be a smart hiker, you need to be ready to survive under any condition.

This book is all about preparing you for emergency hiking situations, and by the time you're finished with it, you'll be ready to face whatever the great outdoors can throw at you!

Chapter 1: How to Prepare for a Hike

No one ever goes on a hike thinking, "Today, I'd like to get lost and spend the weekend wandering around the woods with no food or water." We hear stories of people getting lost all the time, but we never think that it could happen to us. Well, if you're going hiking, you'd better be prepared. A lot goes into preparing for a hike the smart way.

Determine Hike Duration

Before you go on your hike, figure out how long you want to be out there. Perhaps you're just going to walk a trail in the National Forest near your city, or maybe you want to take an overnight hike as you climb a nearby mountain. No matter what type of hike you're planning, make sure that you know how long you plan to be gone.

Why is this important? Simple: if you're gone for too long, your family will know to alert rescue services. This may sound extreme, but you wouldn't be the first person that went for a few-hour hike and got lost - only to return days later. If you want to be sure you're hiking safely, plan to hike for a set time.

Get to Know the Location

You may know a lot about the city in which you live, but how much do you really know about the National Forest, the mountain, or the canyon where you're hiking? Do you know what the wildlife is like or how rough the terrain can be? Do you know if there are sources of fresh water or if there are any navigational landmarks that can help you get home?

You need to learn as much as you can about the place where you are going to hike, as that's the only way to know what you're getting into. Learn about any animals you may encounter - both dangerous and otherwise - and how to deal with them safely. Learn about the terrain you'll be hiking over and take some time to learn the lay of the land. It's the smart way to go, and it will ensure that you can walk away from your hike safely.

Learn the Map

Few people think of bringing a map when walking a trail or climbing a mountain, as they figure that the direction is fairly easy - just "go down," right?

Wrong! You always need to have a map with you as that will help you to find your way back home. Sure, going "down" the mountain will help you to get to the bottom, but how far from your destination will you end up if you go down the wrong side?

Don't bring a road map. It will not help you. Find trail maps that also include topographical futures. Take some time to study your map before you go hiking. Learn the trails that you are supposed to follow and learn about the trail marking system. This will help you to find your way back home if you get lost and learning the map will make it easier for you to visualize the direction you need to take to get back home.

Check the Weather

Do you want to be stuck out on a mountain in a hailstorm? Probably not. Spending a night in the forest with no shelter is rough enough, but imagine how bad it could be if the temperature dropped 20 degrees at night! You need to know what to expect from the weather, as your survival in an emergency situation could depend entirely on a few degrees' change in the weather.

If you can bring a small pocket radio with you on your hike, you can tune in to local weather stations and get the updates on the forecast. You may want to cut your hike short if you hear that it will rain or snow and you should always be prepared for inclement weather before you ever walk out of your front door.

Check your Health

How are you feeling today? Are you energized and invigorated or has a week of work left you tired and fatigued? Are you feeling well, or do you sense the beginnings of a cold or cough coming on? Have any recent injuries healed, or are they still acting up. Take a moment to examine your physical state, as it could make the difference between a great hike and a bad one!

The truth is that you should consider your health carefully before you go on a hike, as it could mean the difference between life and death in some cases. Imagine that you're already coming down with a cold or cough, and then add spending a night or two in the freezing air of the mountain where you're planning to hike. You could end up getting seriously sick! If you have an injury, hiking could just make it worse.

Evaluate how you feel before you ever go on your hike. If you're not feeling 100%, it might be a good idea to postpone the hike.

What You are Going to Wear on Your Hike

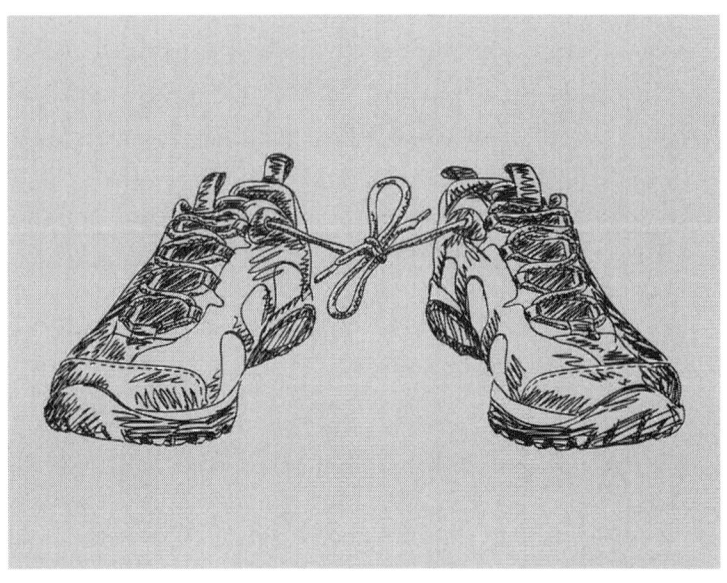

Please, please, please don't wear those blue jeans you love so much. Although it may look like appropriate outfit for hiking, it's not, because it's made from cotton. Cotton is the last possible material you want to wear if you are going to spend night in a wet and cold forest. If cotton gets wet it will take forever to dry it out. I learned it in a hard way and since that I never wear cotton for my hiking trips. There are many special clothes for hiking made of wool and polyester fabrics you can buy.

A lightweight rain jacket by proven manufacturer like Helly Hansen is handy as well. Don't forget about baseball-style hat or wide-brimmed hat for sun protection. Finally, your boots definitely shouldn't be right out of the box. Test your trail shoes ahead of hiking, during your daily routine. Take your hiking outfit seriously. Believe me your outfit may save your life and otherwise.

Check Your Survival Kit

This may sound a bit extreme, but preparing a survival kit is the absolutely MUST thing to do if you are going on a hike. Just packing a water bottle and a walking stick may be good if you're going to walk a 1-mile trail around a city park, but you definitely need to be more seriously prepared if you're going to go trekking or hiking in a wilderness environment.

In a National Forest or Park, there is usually a ranger service that will help you if you get in trouble. However, if you're out in the middle of nowhere, there's no way to receive the emergency medical care or the help you need. Having a survival kit is just the way to go if you're planning on hiking someplace where you'll be on your own.

Make sure your survival kit is properly stocked and check it one last time before heading out the door to be certain that it has everything you need. Your survival kit should be assembled according to your most important needs that could arise if you became lost in a wilderness. We will discuss these survival priorities and your survival kit in more details later in this book.

Think About a Hiking Meal

As you walk, your body burns energy. If you are hiking over rough terrain, you'll end up burning an average of 300 to 400 calories per hour of walking. The average person only has a limited amount of energy available, so walking all day with no food can leave them exhausted, dehydrated, and ravenous.

Water isn't all you'll need- though it is supremely important - you need a bit of food as well. You should bring at least 1,000 calories' worth of food if you plan on hiking for more than 5 hours, as that will give you enough to restore your energy should the hike drag on. You'll also have enough to keep yourself fed in case you get lost and have to spend a few extra hours dragging on.

Chocolate bars, energy bars, protein bars, granola bars, and other sports nutrition bars are nice and compact, and they'll also be a great source of energy. Bring along some food, and you'll decrease your risk of running out of energy in the middle of a hike. Be reasonable, don't overload yourself. In fact, food is not the first priority for short-term survival in the wild.

Prepare a Hiking Plan

If you're going out on a hike, it's wise to prepare a hiking plan. Your plan should include the following:

- Where you are planning on hiking

- The general direction you will be hiking in

- Your destination or the point where you turn around to come home

- The amount of time you estimate it will take

- Where you will be parking your car

Why is this plan so important? Simple, it helps your family know more or less where you are and what you are planning on doing as you are hiking in the wilderness. Leave this hiking plan with them, and they'll know when it's time to call in the emergency rescue services.

Not only will they know when it's time to call for help, but they'll have a general direction and location for them to start. They'll be able to say, "He was going to hike to this destination, and he wanted to walk this path..." This will give the rescue services a place to look for you, ensuring that your rescue will be just that much faster!

Chapter 2: What to Do When You Get Lost

Don't you hate it when you get lost? When you drive around the city, there are so many twists and turns to take to get through the many busy streets. You may end up getting lost easily and finding your way home will be a challenge.

Now, take that feeling of getting lost in the city and multiply it by 100! That's how you'll feel if you're lost out in the middle of nowhere with no idea of where you are or how to get home. It can be an incredibly terrifying feeling to be unsure of where you are or where to walk to return back to civilization, and you may find yourself out in the middle of the wilderness at the end of a long day of hiking with no clue of what to do. If you get this feeling, you are - as the professionals say - "lost."

If you end up lost, there are a several important things you'll need to do. Doing these things will increase your chances of getting out safely!

Don't Panic

This is the first and most important thing to remember if you find that you are lost: **DON'T PANIC!** When you panic - according to Bear Grylls - your brain function is reduced, and you fatigue a lot faster. This means you don't just get tired more quickly, but you're less able to think of a smart plan to rescue yourself.

If you're lost, you're the only person that you can count on to rescue yourself. When you panic, you put yourself in greater danger! Take a moment to breathe, to calm down, and to look around. Think about your options, evaluate your supplies, and see what you can do to make it easier to get out of there alive. If you panic, you're in trouble. If you can stay calm and think rationally, you have a much better chance of getting out safe and sound.

Check Your Map and Compass

Not sure where you are? Before you freak out, pull out that map and take a look at it. A good topographical map will help you to figure out your location according to height and foliage, and you may actually be able to determine a good route home thanks to this map.

A compass is something you should never be without when hiking. You'll be easily able to know where the road, your house, or your car is from your position on the map, and you can follow the compass to lead you back into familiar territory.

Stay Hydrated

The most important things for your survival in an emergency situation may be fire and shelter, but water is definitely next on the list of priorities. If you run out of water, you're going to die in three days or fewer - that's how long your body can survive without water. The only way to survive is to stay hydrated. In normal conditions, your body burns through about 3 to 4 liters of water per day while on a hike, but physical activity, high temperatures, and many other factors can cause your body to use more water. If you're not rehydrating, you could end up in serious trouble - suffering from dehydration.

Your urine is a good marker of your hydration level. Your urine will turn very dark yellow or even brown when your body is running low on water, and it will smell very strong. You will pee much less often, so let your urine be a sign of how dehydrated you are. If you can find water, do so immediately! You need a good source of water and refill your water supplies. Here are some useful tips to help you stave off dehydration?

- Suck on a rock. It's a bit dangerous, but it can help to keep your mouth producing enough saliva. Just don't swallow it!

- Stay away from salt. If you've brought salty food with you, don't eat it if you don't have water. Salt just dries your body out even more!

- Breathe through your nose. It will stop your mouth from drying out.

The sooner you can find more water to drink, the better!

Stay Warm

If you're out in the middle of nowhere when night falls, you're going to get pretty cold at night. Even if you're living in the desert, the nights can get pretty chilly - not to mention the wind chill factor. Staying warm is the key to surviving through the rough nights out in the wild.

To stay warm:

- Wear a hat. A lot of your body heat escapes through your head, but a hat will trap it and keep it close to your body - keeping you nice and warm.

- Take off damp clothing. If your socks, shoes, or clothes are wet, the dampness will soak into your body and make you colder. It's smart to take off any wet clothing, and you'll feel so much better without those damp items.

- Start a fire. If you can start a fire, it will warm you up AND boost your morale. It's smart to include fire-starting materials in your survival kit and always keep an eye out for debris you can use to make a fire at night.

- Eat and drink. When your body processes food, the digestion process produces energy or calories that can keep your body warm. You'll find that having a little snack and a drink can help to warm you up nicely.

- Exercise. It may not help you to sleep, but jumping and moving around can help to wake you up and warm you up!

- Block the wind. Your shelter needs to keep out the wind as much as possible, as the wind chill drops the temperature even further!

- Stuff your clothes. Find hay, leaves, dried grass, and anything else that will act as an insulator to keep you warm at night. Stuff that into your clothes, and, as uncomfortable as it may be, you'll definitely be a lot warmer.

- Get something under you. Your body heat will be absorbed into the ground as you sleep, so putting a layer between yourself and the ground is the key to staying warm at night.

Staying warm is the key to a good night's sleep, which could make a difference if you're trying to find your way home!

Build Yourself a Shelter

One of the most important thing to help you survive: a shelter.

A shelter will keep the rain off your head and can protect you from a very hot sun as well. It will block the wind and can protect you from animals. Building a shelter can be fairly easy if you have lots of materials, but a lack of materials can make it very hard!

For your shelter:

- Use a rock, fallen tree, or any other large objects as the base of your shelter. It gives you something sturdy for support.

- Look for large branches, which will form the "rafters" or "beams" of your shelter. Lay them next to each other, as close together as possible.

- Use smaller branches, leaves, and grass to windproof the shelter as much as possible.

The less wind that can get into your shelter at night, the warmer you'll be!

You'd be amazed at what you can use to make yourself a shelter, and you have so many types of shelters to choose from:

- A lean-to

- An A-frame

- A poncho tent

- Teepee

- Tree bed

- Debris hut

These are just a few, but there are many more. Look around you, use what you can find and make the best shelter you can!

Have a Way to Signal Rescuers

If you are lost, you need to think that someone will be looking for you. Your family has your hiking plan, so they'll know how long to wait before calling the emergency rescuing services. With the right signaling method, you'll make finding you much easier!

What can you use to signal?

- **Fire**. Start a fire at night, and it will be visible for miles. If you need to start a fire during the day, add lots of green branches - which will produce a lot of dark smoke.

- **Flares.** If you can bring a few flares with you, you'll be easily able to signal for a rescue. Even pen flares will work.

- **Whistle.** Good whistle will be heard from far away and alert rescuers to your position.

- **Shiny Objects.** The back of your Smartphone can act as a mirror, which can be used to reflect light as a signal. You can also use your canteen, a belt buckle, or anything else metallic. It's better to have tiny glass mirror in your survival kit as it can send strong signal for several miles.

With a way to send up a signal, you'll increase the chances that you will be rescued.

Chapter 3: Build Your Own Basic Survival Kit

If you're going hiking, you're going to need a basic survival kit to help you make it through any emergency situation you find yourself in. You should build the survival kit according to survival necessities that we've discussed in previous chapter. You'd be amazed at how compact your survival kit can be and yet you'll still have all that you need to survive in any situation.

This survival kit will cost you a bit of money, but it's totally worth it. You may never end up using the items in the kit, but it's better to have them and not need them, right? With a good hard case to protect your items, you're ready for a hike!

What goes into a good survival kit?

Compass

A compass is probably the most important thing to add to your survival kit. With a compass, you should be able to guide yourself home easily. It is incredibly simple to learn to read a compass, and the device will make it easy to get yourself back to civilization no matter how lost you are!

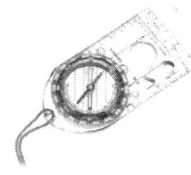

There are many items with a built-in compass around. You can even buy a whistle with built in compass, but I would prefer more trustworthy device as soon as my survival depends on it. My choice is Suunto M3D Leader Compass. It is simple base-plate model designed for North America and has everything for quality backcountry navigation. Weight: 1.6 oz.

First Aid Kit

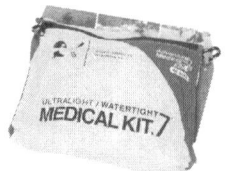

Don't bring an entire pharmacy on your hiking trip. A simple survival first aid kit will come with bandages, hydrogen peroxide, iodine, braces for injured wrists and ankles, and a few other simple things. You will find that having these few items will make treating any injury a whole lot easier! I use one of those prepackaged kits by Adventure Medical Kits. It is functional, light, and watertight. I just made some additions like insect repellent and a sunscreen. Don't forget to include your personal prescription medication. Weight: 8 oz.

Gloves

You don't want to have to use your entire medical kit to repair your hands after building a shelter, gathering firewood, and starting a fire, so bring gloves. Heavy duty leather gloves from the nearest hardware store will be just fine. I use Mechanix Coyote Gloves. Weight: 3.2 oz.

Signaling Devices

Most hikers like to use a whistle as a means of signaling, and it will definitely come in handy if there are people around. Get one that is used by referees since you can hear it over the roar of 50,000 crazy fans. Fox40 model, for example, is a good choice. Weight: 1oz. You should also include a tiny signal mirror. Weight: 0.5 oz.

Water Purification Tablets and Water Filters

There are dozens of tablets to help you purify your water, and you can find them in just about every store where outdoor and camping goods are sold. You should try them at home to determine if your stomach can handle it. I carry Katadyn Micropur Purification Tablets in my survival kit, but personally I prefer using Life Straw Water Filter. This device has been tested by University of Arizona to meet the EPA's filtration standards. It removes 99.9999% of bacteria. Weight: 2 oz.

Energy Bars

Energy bars may not taste like a gourmet meal, but they're very portable and will supply your body with all necessary nutrients for a few days. They'll help to restore your energy, as they're packed with calories. I usually pack four Kate's Grizzly Bars, which will result in 1,500 calories and 12 oz. weight.

Blanket

A good emergency survival kit should always have a blanket - a thermal blanket, to be precise. They're compact and very lightweight, but they do a great job of trapping heat near your body! I recommend using SOL heat sheets Survival Blanket by AMK that reflects up to 90% of radiated body heat. It is also tear resistant so you can use it for shelter building and rain protection. It is also reusable in comparison with other blankets. Weight: 3.2 oz.

Fire Starting Tools

A pack of waterproof matches in a watertight bag may be just the thing to help you get that fire lit, but in my opinion, a good old fashioned Bic Lighter is much better choice. In a real survival situation, a good reliable lighter is able to start a lot more fires than those few matches.

You should also consider buying a flint and steel. There are many fire-starting devices that you can buy online or in stores, and you'll find that they're definitely going to make your life a whole lot easier. The only thing, you should test those devices before your hiking trip to be absolutely sure that you are equipped with dependable fire starter. In my kit I have a Fire Steel spark rod and cotton balls with petroleum jelly Vaseline in a waterproof case. Total weight is 2.3 oz.

Knife

A Swiss Army Knife is one of the best tools you can have in your survival kit. Leatherman Multi-Tool will do the job as well. Even if you just have a simple knife, it will be enough to keep you alive!

You'll be able to clean any food you catch, protect yourself in the wild, cut branches for building a shelter, and so much more! My personal preference is light-weight folding knife Spyderco Delica 4. It is my favorite because of its super reliability and high quality. Weight: 2.5 oz.

Flashlight

A small flashlight can be the difference between stumbling around in the dark and an easy way home. A pen flashlight may not be very powerful, but it's easily portable. When choosing a flashlight, pay attention to light output, battery ran time, water resistance, size, and weight. In my kit, I carry Fenix PD35 Flashlight that has a good balance between small size, stunning 850-lumen brightness and reasonable runtime. Weight: 3.1 oz.

A good LED headlamp can also help make your trip a whole lot easier although it is not absolutely necessary for a basic survival kit. My favorite is Princeton Tec Corona LED Headlamp that provides very bright flood and excellent peripheral light. Weight: 8 oz. Don't forget about spare batteries for all those devices.

Spare Prescription Glasses

If you are wearing prescription glasses, you probably already have the habit of never leave home without spare. Put one in your survival kit as well.

With these things, you're definitely going to be in much better shape no matter how "lost" you get!

Chapter 4: Three Essentials to Wilderness Survival

You may find yourself in a survival situation for any number of reasons. You might get lost while hiking, your car might break down far from any assistance— your imagination won't have any trouble coming up with how it could happen. As bad as it might seem in the moment, there's truly little to worry about if you simply use your head and remember to make the best possible use of the items you have on you at the time. While having the survival kit is very important, knowing how to use the different items in your kit is just as important. All of the gear will do you no good if you don't know how to use it, and it will just add extra weight.

There are three things of vital importance: fire, water, and a knowledge of the basic principles of land navigation. After you've finished this book, you need to get yourself outside and practice the skills you've learned. The knowledge is a must, but knowledge without experience is of very limited value.

How many times have you watched reality television shows and seen individuals fail miserably at producing fire? It's funny to watch from your warm and comfortable living room, but not knowing how to apply the basic skills is suicide in the wilderness. In this book we will cover the basic knowledge and skills required for you to survive under primitive conditions.

Fire: The Importance of Keeping Warm

The human body must maintain a core temperature of at least 95° Fahrenheit to prevent going into a state of hypothermia. At the onset of hypothermia, your pulse rate slows, your pupils dilate, your speech becomes slurred, and you start to lose muscle control. Any of these signs is serious and requires that you find some way to raise your core temperature. Shivering and chattering teeth are autonomic responses that actually generate heat from your body, so they are no cause for concern.

If no action is taken that raises your core temperature, you begin to get sleepy, which is the last stage of hypothermia before death. Once your core temperature drops below 82.3° Fahrenheit, your body can't be revived. Have I got your attention now?

Always make sure you are dressed properly for your activity and location. Loose, baggy clothes are better for both warmth and cold, and it's easier to take off that sweater or jacket and tie it around your waist than to produce one that you simply didn't bring with you.

Keep in mind that using natural terrain features, trees, caves, a gully, a ditch, or even just a dip in the ground can get you out of the heat-stealing wind. Any kind of shelter you can fabricate will make staying alive that much easier. Getting out of the wind also causes your fire to require less fuel, and you'll get a better return on the energy you use to collect fuel.

Getting wet increases your risk of hypothermia, since moisture wicks off your skin, stealing calories of heat as it does so. Make every effort to stay dry; don't try to sleep in clothes that are wet from being immersed, rained on, or perspired in, and take every opportunity to dry out wet clothing. Special care should be taken to make sure that you keep your socks dry and rub your feet to encourage circulation. The old adage that you lose most of your body heat through your head has been proven false—an exposed head will account for only 7–10% of your total heat loss.

Keeping yourself warm, and therefore alive, is essential to survival in the wild. Warmth alone, vital as it is, would be reason enough to learn the art of starting a fire, but there are other benefits to having a fire as well. You can use fire to cook food, purify the water that is second in importance on your survival necessities list, keep wild animals away, and help to keep bothersome insects at bay. Best of all, it can be used as a signal to those who might be searching for you.

Fire Basics

Three things are required to produce fire: fuel, oxygen and tinder. Oxygen is everywhere around you, so there is no need to explain its use or how to acquire it. We'll discuss the other two to give you a thorough understanding of what they are and how to acquire them.

Fuel

Fuel is normally determined by your environment. Hardwood (from leaf-bearing trees) is best for warmth and lasts the longest. Softwoods, from needle-bearing trees, is next best and is often a good choice when you are trying to keep insects and animals at bay. It burns faster and leaves a sap residue on your hands and clothing. Next comes heavy grasses or brush, and finally, paper. If you are in a desert or prairie environment, you may be forced to use dried animal dung—but don't worry, the bacteria is dead and gone long before the dung is dry enough to burn. Find the driest fuel available. If there has been a light rain, try digging under the leaves on the ground. Wet fuel is much harder to burn, though it is possible to use enough kindling to dry it out sufficiently to burn well. Once the larger, thicker fuel is burning well, you can use wetter logs to burn.

Kindling and Tinder

Kindling is just smaller fuel, ranging from dry twigs (as small as you can find) up to dry sticks an inch in diameter. Dryness is key to the success of kindling, unless you are fortunate enough to have a solid fuel tablets stashed away in your first-aid kit (which is actually a really good idea). Always start with as fine or thin a material as you can find for kindling wood. The flame generated by tinder is usually minimal, and you may have to blow on the embers for a long time to get the kindling to flame up. Blowing on the glowing embers adds oxygen to the mix and causes the embers to flare up into flames.

Tinder is the driest, most flammable material you can find. If you have a magnesium stick in your survival kit, you can use magnesium as a tinder. Scrape off some of the magnesium with a knife, put it in a little pile and use the knife and the flint side to light the magnesium, it burns really hot and lights almost anything.

If you don't have magnesium, anything that will flame up from a spark landing on it will work. A piece of dry facial or bathroom tissue, cotton balls, dandelion florets, and dry, crackly leaves work well as tinder, as do any form of newspaper or other thin paper product. Wood shavings (cut from a dry stick), birds' nests, strings shredded from a shoe lace, and anything that is light and dry will work; use your imagination. Use as much as you can, as this is the critical point of building any fire. You must be able to get your tinder to burn with a small spark or ember in order to make your fire burn.

Once the spark is glowing, gentle puffs of air will cause the tinder to blaze.

Types of Survival Fire

Starting any type of fire in the wild requires that you clear, to bare dirt, an area at least ten feet in diameter. Running from a forest fire is an exercise in futility and should be avoided at all costs. If at all possible, you should surround your fire with rocks, but if that is not possible, scrape a hole in the ground or scrape an earthen berm around it. Lay your fire by building layers, setting the tinder down first, stacking the kindling above it, and finally, the fuel on top. Three basic types of survival fires are cook fires, fires to maintain heat, and signal fires.

Cook fires should be small, hot-burning, nearly smokeless fires that are easy to reach over and around. A large fire or one that is too tall is extremely difficult to cook on and is one of the leading causes of injuries in camping and wilderness survival.

Fires to maintain heat should be low, thick, wide, and preferably built against some rock face that will reflect the heat back towards you. Scraping dirt out of the ground and building an earthen berm behind the fire will not be as effective as using a stone wall, but it will still reflect heat back on you and make better use of your available fuel. Any combination of earth, stone, or logs will work fine.

Signal fires should be high and throw off significant light. Green boughs from a needle-bearing tree should be heaped on a daytime signal fire to send a cloud of visible smoke into the air for rescuers to see.

Methods of Starting a Fire

Tinder can be lit by using a lens and sunlight. The lens can be a magnifying glass, a thick piece of broken bottle glass—any type of glass that refracts light into a concentrated point. Holding the glass at a distance from the tinder that allows the light to be concentrated to its smallest point, keep the pinpoint of light steady in one place until the tinder begins to smoke. If flames do not start of their own volition, blow gently on the smoking tinder until the flames sprout. Then add kindling until your fire is large enough to burn fuel.

Flint and steel is another way to start a fire. The preparation of tinder, kindling, and fuel is the same, though extra care must be taken in selecting dry and easily flammable tinder. Many devices are commercially available just for this purpose, and they're easily carried in a pocket or first aid kit. Even if you don't have such a device available, you still can start fire by this method using just common pocket knife. If there is no flint readily available, chcrt or jasper will work as well. Flint can be located on or around most limestone or chalk outcroppings. Holding the flint firmly in your weak hand, strike sharply downward with your steel, causing sparks to cascade onto your tinder. At the first sign of a glow or tendril of smoke, blow on the tinder until flames sprout from it, then feed it kindling until the fire will burn fuel. This method of fire-starting needs a loose-jointed wrist and some practice.

There are many more primitive methods of fire starting. It would be best to find one or two that are the most comfortable for you and practice them until you are adept at the craft. In any event, it would be far wiser to make sure you always have matches or a butane lighter either in your pocket or in your first aid kit at all times. If you are using matches, make sure to protect them from the rain and wind. Strike the matches as close to the kindling as possible, so as to prevent them from being blown out. Put the match straight into a pile of kindling and protect the kindling until it lights. Birch bark is a proven kindling even under the wet conditions.

If you or someone with you has an accelerant of some sort—alcohol, acetone (such as nail polish remover), oil, Vaseline (either the jelly or the lip balm)—use them. The Esbit hexamine solid fuel tablets illustrated here are inexpensive, and will work even with wet wood under the most extreme weather conditions. Each fuel tablet is 1.0 x 1.5 x 0.5 inches and weighs only 14 grams. They slip easily into a first aid kit and take up little room.

Survival is a pass/fail subject, and there is no such thing as cheating. Practice fire-building in as many different conditions as possible. If you are confident in your fire-starting ability in any situation and you have the proven kit, your chances of surviving in the wild are multiplying.

Water

Exposure is your first concern in a survival situation. Your second concern is water. It may be uncomfortable to be hungry, but the human body can last for three weeks or more without food, depending upon your energy expenditure and body mass. Without water, you can expect to last three to five days—again, depending on your environment.

The drier the air, the greater your fluid loss, regardless of the ambient temperature.

Your best bets to retain fluids are to avoid exertion, breathe through your nose, and don't drink your water ration. Take small sips of your water and hold it in your mouth as long as you can before swallowing it. The Plains Indians used to place small pebbles in their mouths to keep their saliva glands secreting moisture in the mouth. It's an old trick, but it's very effective.

Finding Water

Locating water is mostly a matter of common sense. Always watch the local fauna. All mammals require water, and they generally make trails as they follow the paths from their foraging areas to their drinking water source. The presence of bees is an absolute indicator of a nearby water source; follow them.

Artesian springs are generally safe to drink from. Streams fed by artesian springs that run over a sandy bottom purify themselves every ten feet and are generally safe to drink from unless there are cultivated fields nearby. Even though these streams and springs look clear, smell sweet, and even taste decent, it can't hurt to use water purification tablets to ensure there are no biological contaminants.

Look in low areas if obvious sources are not available, keeping an eye out for clumps of overly green plants or reeds—if you need to dig for water, these are all indicators of water near the surface.

Producing Water: Condensation Method

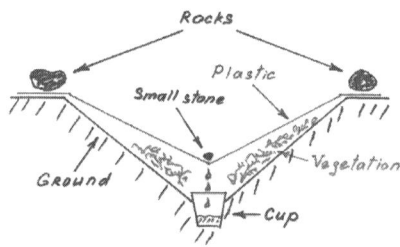

In more arid areas, you can use the condensation method to obtain drinking water. This method requires a sheet of clear plastic, either sheet plastic such as Visqueen or thin plastic such as Saran Wrap. Seek the low ground where plants are growing, or better yet, the low points of a dry creek bed— somewhere that's fully in sunshine. Scoop out a cone-shaped hole about three feet across and fifteen inches deep. Plant a collection vessel at the apex of the cone. Stacking lush vegetation around the walls of the cone will provide more moisture and aid in condensation as the sun raises the temperature under the plastic.

The plastic is used to cover the top of the hole, sealed tightly with rocks and/or soil, and weighted down in the center with a weight or another small stone. The low point of the plastic should be just above the center of the receptacle, so that the condensed water drips into it.

Depending on the moisture in the soil and in the vegetation you put inside, this still will produce one to four pints of pure water per day. There are other methods of trapping condensation requiring more articles than you'll likely be carrying on a hike or in your first aid kit. The inflatable solar kits tend to be expensive and large, and therefore unlikely to be carried on a short hike. The water obtained by this method is absolutely pure and doesn't require boiling or water purification tablets.

Filtration

Discolored or silty water may be all that you have available for drinking. Letting the water stand for twelve hours in some kind of container will make the discoloration go away, but you would still need to use water purification tablets to make it potable. Filtration systems provide a means to clarify and purify water.

Check the illustration for a simple, field-expedient filter you can construct with a two liter plastic bottle or with a plastic milk jug. These containers can frequently be found discarded almost anywhere.

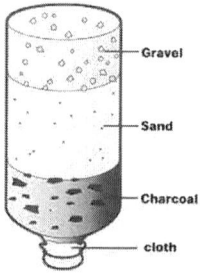

Place the cloth at the neck of the bottle. It can be almost any kind of cloth—the finer, the better. You can cut out material from a shirt without destroying its value to you as clothing. The charcoal can be obtained from your campfire. Pick up the coals from your fire and shake off the ash. Place the black charcoal on a flat surface and pulverize it, leaving no large pieces. The charcoal should be fairly uniform in size, about like rough sand. Put the pulverized charcoal above the cloth in the container until it is about a third full. Use your fist or the flat end of a stick to pack the charcoal down tightly.

Put the finest sand you can get in the next third of the container, if you can locate any. This step is not absolutely necessary, but it will definitely improve the quality and taste of the water you produce. The top third of the container should be filled with fine gravel, but grasses or moss can be used as substitutes.

When your filter is complete, simply pour water in the top until it begins to overflow, and then hold the neck over your collection vessel. If there is any discoloration left in the water you filter, simply run the water back through the filter again as often as necessary until the water is clear and has no bad taste.

Charcoal is the essential ingredient in even your municipal filtration system and will remove all but the most pernicious of toxins from your filtered water. It is still advisable to use water purification tablets, if you have them, to ensure that all biological and chemical contaminants have been neutralized.

Filtration Devices

Recent developments in personal water purification devices have revolutionized the art. Handy, simple, and very portable, these items can be worn on a string around your neck and used whenever you find a source of water. Their particulate screens are so fine that they can separate even the smallest microorganisms that contaminate water—even viruses.

The Lifestraw is the first of these. Simple to use, just uncap both ends and stick the thicker end in the water source. Suck in enough water to fill and prime the unit and let it sit for a few minutes, and then you can drink your fill directly from the water source. The unit is good for purifying a thousand liters of contaminated water.

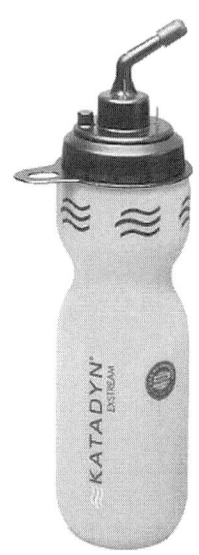

The second development is the personal drinking cup purifier. Several manufacturers produce similar products, and most of them are extremely effective. These devices can screen minute organisms down to the size of viruses as well, and they're so portable that you don't appear to be a lunatic when you wear one around your neck on a hike. There should be at least one of these in your vehicle when you go out of town, and since you can use it with fresh water as well as bad, they're not out of place on a hiking trail either.

Water Purification Tablets

Water purification tablets are inexpensive and commercially available. The bottles are usually small and easily packable and transportable. Water purification tablets are your insurance policy. They neutralize even biological contaminants and ensure that your water is perfectly safe.

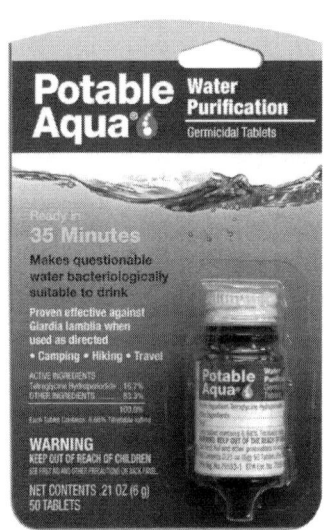

The drawback is that they do not remove suspended particles or offensive odors. Either the charcoal filter or distilling will accomplish those things for you. Using the tablets is simply a matter of dropping a couple of the tablets into a container and shaking it up, then waiting for the time specified in the instructions before drinking. Once again, these tablets will not make the water clear or remove bad odors; they simply neutralize toxins and kill bacteria.

Boiling water

If you don't have any of the above tools, boil the water to kill off the germs. OK, you can start a fire because you've mastered this skill, but where you are going to get a pot? You can make a container out of tree bark. It is impossible to put this pot on a fire, but you can heat a stone in the hot coals and then put it into the container with water. It will be enough to boil the water. Again you better practice this trick well before you find yourself struggling in the wild.

Land Navigation: To Move or not to Move

The cardinal rule of survival is "use your head." The first question you need to ask yourself is whether it is wiser to stay where you are or make an effort to walk out. If you are the survivor of an aircraft crash, don't move. Rescue operations will be searching for the wreckage, not combing the wilderness for survivors. If your location is known to friends and relatives, you are probably safer to stay where you are.

If you need to walk out, you absolutely have to have some knowledge of the area. It doesn't help to know in which direction north lies if you have no idea of the location of the roads in the area or where they lead to. Even if you have the latest in lensatic compasses in your survival kit, without a detailed topographical map, the compass is serious overkill. So, when it comes to navigation, a compass and topographic map together are your best friends.

In a situation that you don't have any of these tools, but you've studied the map before your trip, you need to determine the cardinal directions. You simply need to locate where magnetic north is. The stories you were told as a child about moss only growing on the north side of a tree are entirely untrue. Determining the basic cardinal directions is very simple and you can do it by a number of simple methods. We will deal with three of the simplest methods here: the Shadow Tip Method, the Watch Method, and Celestial Navigation.

Shadow Tip Method

The Shadow Tip method is extremely simple. All you require is a level spot in the sunshine, a stick about a yard long, and two distinctive items to mark the tip of the stick's shadow on the ground. Drive the stick perpendicular to the ground and mark the top of its shadow by marking the dirt or placing a marker on the ground. This mark will always be west, no matter where on Earth you are located.

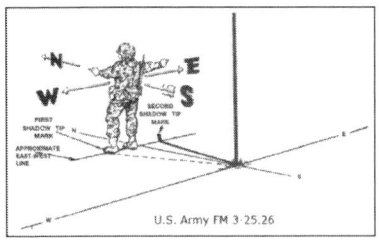

U.S. Army FM 3-25.26

Wait a minimum of fifteen minutes and then mark the shadow's tip again in the same manner as before. Draw a line from the first marker to the second marker. This line, with the first marker to your left, is the east-west line. Perpendicular to this line is the north-south line, with north being straight ahead and west (the first mark) being to your left. The illustration is from U.S. Army FM 3-25.26 Map Reading and Land Navigation.

The Watch Method

In order to make the watch method work, you must make certain that your watch is not set on daylight savings time. Hold your watch flat in your hand and point the hour hand directly towards the sun. Looking at the face of the watch, bisect the angle created by the hour hand and the 12 on the watch face, and you will establish your north-south baseline.

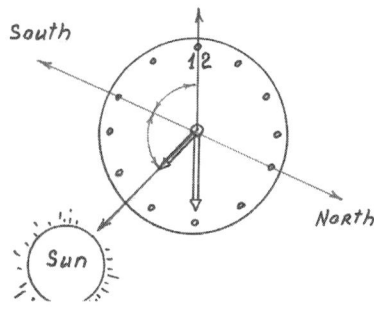

Check the sun to determine whether it is in the east (before noon) or in the west (afternoon), then orient yourself so your left shoulder is facing west. Straight ahead will be north. If you have a digital watch, simply draw the current time on a watch face on paper and use it just as you would a watch.

This only works in the Northern Hemisphere; in the Southern Hemisphere, point the 12 o'clock mark at the sun and bisect the angle between it and the hour hand to get the north-south baseline.

Celestial Navigation

In our case, Celestial Navigation means nothing more than locating the North Star. The axis of the Earth is pointed almost directly at the North Star, or Polaris, and therefore it seems to never move. Polaris is the last star in the handle of Ursa Minor, commonly called the Little Dipper.

The Little Dipper can always be located by using the front two stars of the Big Dipper, which is probably the easiest of all the celestial signs to recognize. Extend a line through the front two stars of the familiar Big Dipper, and you have what amounts to an arrow pointing at Polaris.

Mental Attitude

More than anything else, you need a survival attitude in order to survive. Look around for things that you can use to protect and shelter yourself while out in the wild and always be on the lookout for food and water sources. Keep an ear out for any signs of human life and be prepared to be rescued. Keep up that positive attitude that you will be found, and never, ever give up hope. Always push forward and keep working on making your way home. Most of the time, you're the only one that will rescue yourself!

Chapter 5: Your Best Friend When Lost - Personal Location Beacon

If you're going hiking and there's even the slightest chance that you'll get lost, you should definitely get yourself a personal locator beacon. These devices are basically like GPS devices that let others know where you are, making it possible to find you no matter where you are or how lost you get.

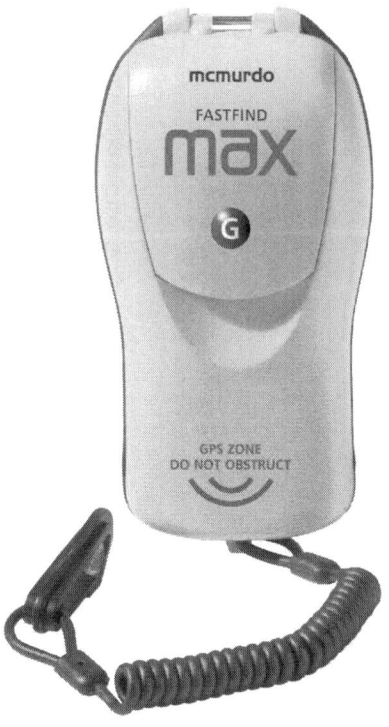

I prefer McMurdo Fast Find Max G model. This waterproof unit is guaranteed to work for 48 hours after you activated it. This is quite expensive equipment and also quite heavy at 10 ounces, but these beacons can be your ticket out of the wilderness or an emergency situation. Remember that you should be very careful using this device, because activating it by mistake will trigger erroneous and expensive rescue attempts.

These beacons are made to be activated if you get lost, and they'll keep broadcasting your signal as you hike. The signal will be sent via satellite, and it will be broadcast to all emergency services in the area. They're built in a durable, waterproof case that is very damage-resistant, so there's very little risk of the beacon being damaged.

When you buy the beacon, you're supposed to register it with local emergency services. The beacon will then be connected to the database and satellite service that will help to locate you should you get lost, and all you need to do is activate it.

Some beacons use a GPS device, and these devices can lead rescuers to within 100 meters of your position. If you use the cheaper devices, they're without GPS, and will only lead rescuers to within 2 miles of your position. Either way, both devices increase your chances of being saved!

Conclusion

We have just scratched the surface of the wilderness survival topic. We have just discussed the very basic and critical survival skills. They are not the only skills you need, but without these skills, you won't live long enough to worry about the others.

The most important tip you should take away from this book is that you should never travel without the survival kit that contains some carefully thought out survival items. It's easier to have something and not need it than to need something and not have it.

Good Luck and Good Hiking!

Thank You

Thank you for taking time to read "Hiking Survival Guide". If you enjoyed it, please consider telling your friends or posting a short review on Hiking Survival Guide Amazon page. Word of mouth is an author's best friend and much appreciated.

Conrad Blake is pleased to introduce his new book.

This book is for anyone looking to improve their life with a form of relaxation that has many benefits to those who can use it properly!

The daily practice of meditation is scientifically proven to help you to be happier, experience less depression, be healthier and be better balanced in all areas of your life!

Once you begin to meditate you will notice the beneficial effects in your work, at home and in your relationships. You will feel more relaxed and happy with your life and your days will become full of fun again!

Meditating regularly can help you to focus your energies and can get you away from the stresses that we all experience on a daily basis.

"How to Meditate - A Beginner's Guide" will show you how to master the elusive art of meditation, in an easy to understand way.

Printed in Poland
by Amazon Fulfillment
Poland Sp. z o.o., Wrocław